UNIVERSITY OF OXFORD
ASHMOLEAN MUSEUM

ARTHUR EVANS, KNOSSOS AND THE PRIEST-KING

by

S. SHERRATT

ASHMOLEAN MUSEUM · OXFORD
2000

Fig. 1. Four-sided sealstone with hieroglyphic signs, presented to the Ashmolean by Greville Chester in 1889 (Ashmolean Museum 1889.998). Though it supposedly came from Sparta, by 1894 Evans was convinced that it must really be from Crete.

Arthur Evans, Knossos and the Priest-King

Almost exactly a century ago, on 23rd March 1900, Arthur Evans began excavating at the site of Knossos, thus bringing to fruition six years of determined planning and waiting. It seems likely that he had made up his mind that the site was worth investigating before he set eyes on it in spring 1894, on his first visit to Crete. The previous summer, his young friend John L. Myres, then Craven Scholar at the University of Oxford, had visited the island with Evans's encouragement, after together they had found sealstones engraved with pictographic or hieroglyphic signs, said to be from Crete, among the wares of the antiquities dealers of Athens. Evans's interest in the possibility of prehistoric Aegean scripts had been further roused by a sealstone given to the Ashmolean by the Revd Greville Chester in 1889 (Fig. 1), and as a result of conversations with the Italian epigraphist Federico Halbherr, whom he had met in Rome in 1892 and who was well acquainted with the antiquities of Crete, he was already more than part-way convinced that evidence of the earliest European writing was to be sought on the island, probably among some more highly developed civilisation than that of the Mycenaeans which had begun to be uncovered on the Greek mainland some twenty years earlier. Myres himself wrote back glowingly of various sites on Crete and particularly of Knossos, where he hoped "to have a dig there next season, if the influential natives will let me; but they would rather leave the things underground than suffer anything to go by compact to Constantinople".[1]

As it happened, the "influential natives" were not at all keen on letting Myres, a relatively penniless and untried youngster, excavate at Knossos. The potential importance of the site, otherwise known as Kephala or "Ta Pitharia", from the fragments of pithoi or large storage jars which littered its surface along with the remains of stone walls, had been appreciated for some time. In 1878–9, the aptly named Minos Kalokairinos, a local merchant and brother of the British Vice-Consul in Heraklion, Lysimachos Kalokairinos, had made a number of soundings in what was eventually to turn out to be the West Wing of the Palace, and recovered pieces of pottery and some large pithoi, one of which found its way to the British Museum. Foreign archaeologists had also shown an interest. Heinrich Schliemann, the uncoverer of Homer's Troy and Mycenae, had expressed a wish to dig at Knossos as early as 1883, and, though he got as far as negotiating to buy the site on a visit to the island in 1885, he eventually withdrew, defeated by the high price demanded by its wily Turkish proprietors. The French School at Athens, in the person of André Joubin, had also shown itself eager to dig there, and was still actively pursuing this enthusiasm. However, Crete in the early 1890s, though restive, was still part of the Ottoman empire and it was inevitable, under current Ottoman legislation, that as soon as

Fig. 2. View of Kephala hill, Knossos, from south, during excavations of 1900.

anything worthwhile emerged from the soil of Knossos it would be removed to the Imperial Museums in Constantinople – something that the Cretan intellectual establishment, among them Joseph Hazzidakis, the President of the Heraklion Syllogos (an educational association concerned with preserving the cultural and antiquarian heritage of ancient and Christian Crete) were keen to avoid at all costs.

From this point of view, Myres, as a young man of untried views and without political influence and connections, must have seemed a poor risk. Evans, however, whose political credentials as a supporter of the Christian Orthodox cause had been proved impeccable by his earlier activities as political correspondent in the Balkans,[2] succeeded where Myres (and the Turcophile Joubin) had failed in persuading Hazzidakis to support his aim of excavating at Knossos. By the time his first visit to Crete ended in April 1894 he had come to an agreement

with Hazzidakis to purchase a quarter share of the land on his behalf, with the idea that this would give him a lever for eventually acquiring the whole of the site. The fulfilment of his aims, however, had to wait for another six years, riding out various legal obstacles placed in his way by the intractable (and often elusive) owners of the rest of the land in 1896, and further sustained uprisings in 1897–8 when control of the island was taken over by a Consortium of the Great Powers of Britain, France, Italy and Russia.[3] Crete eventually gained independence under the nominal rule of the Sultan at the end of 1898, the Turkish troops were withdrawn, many of the Turkish inhabitants abandoned the island, and Prince George of Greece took over as High Commissioner. He it was who gave Evans the final go-ahead to start at Knossos. Hazzidakis successfully completed the final purchase of the whole site on Evans's behalf at the beginning of 1900, and the excavations began not long after.

4

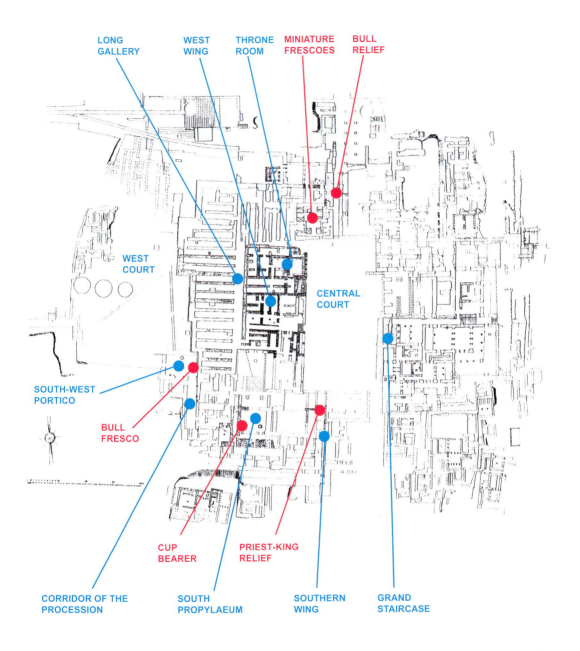

LONG GALLERY

WEST WING

THRONE ROOM

MINIATURE FRESCOES

BULL RELIEF

WEST COURT

CENTRAL COURT

SOUTH-WEST PORTICO

BULL FRESCO

CUP BEARER

PRIEST-KING RELIEF

CORRIDOR OF THE PROCESSION

SOUTH PROPYLAEUM

SOUTHERN WING

GRAND STAIRCASE

Fig. 3. Plan of the Knossos Palace, based on M.S.F. Hood and W. Taylor, The Bronze Age Palace at Knossos. Plan and sections *(London, 1981).*

Fig. 4. Photograph of Throne Room, as excavated in 1900, showing patches of fresco decoration still clinging to the walls. The remains of a griffin were found fallen forward in front of the far wall, to the right of Arthur Evans.

The first season, which lasted for over three months, from 23rd March until the hot weather set in at the beginning of June, was concentrated on the highest point of the Kephala hill, in the area now known as the West Wing of the Palace, west of the Central Court (Figs. 2, 3). It was a truly productive season. On 30th March the first linear inscribed clay tablet was found, and this was followed by further plentiful finds of similar tablets and by a number of tablets inscribed in the "hieroglyphic" script which had first attracted Evans's attention to Crete. Most of the West Wing was uncovered, including the West Court, the South-West Portico and entrance (later renamed the West Portico), the South Propylaeum, the Long Gallery flanked by storage magazines, part of the Central Court and, of course, the famous Throne Room, with its intact gypsum throne and the remains of fresco decoration still clinging to the walls (Fig. 4). The recovery of painted fresco fragments was, indeed, a most notable feature of this season, and one which – together with the inscribed tablets – drew particular excitement and satisfaction from Evans. Among the first to be found, in the first few days of excavation, were some fragments with simple dot-rosette decoration from the remains of a house lying on the south-east slope of the hill, outside the palace. However, within the palace itself, fragments of miniature fresco showing the remains of a painted shrine were found in a room to the north, while from an adjacent area came the head of a charging bull, ex-

6

ecuted in a relief technique (Fig. 5). The remains of another life-sized figure of a bull, this time painted flat, were found in the area of the South-West Portico, and just to the east of this, in a corridor named by Evans the Corridor of the Procession, were found the remains of a series of large human figures in richly embroidered robes, which Evans characterised as "princely, priestly or official personages".[4] Among these were the remains of the lower parts of female figures in flounced robes, one of whom Evans was inclined to identify as a Queen (Fig. 6). On the 5th April, somewhat to the east of this, in the area given the name of the South Propylaeum, came the most exciting fresco find of all: two large pieces, lying on the ground where they had fallen from the wall, which revealed a virtually intact life-size figure (minus the legs, but including the head and face) which carried in its hand a funnel-shaped cup or rhyton (Fig. 7). This figure, which was eventually christened the Cup-Bearer, afforded the first portrayal to be

Fig. 5. Head of a bull, executed in relief, found in 1900 in the area of the Northern Entrance Passage.

unearthed of an inhabitant of prehistoric Knossos, and in his report of the 1900 excavations, published in the *Annual of the British School at Athens*, Evans notes that its "regular, almost classical features, the dark eyes and black curly hair and high brachycephalic skull present close points of resemblance to certain types still to be found, especially in the highlands of central and western Crete. The profile rendering of the eye and the modelling of the face and limbs show an artistic advance which in historic

Fig. 6. E. Gilliéron père's reconstruction drawing of part of the Procession Fresco, showing the figure characterised by Evans in 1900 as a "Queen", distinguished as female by her white feet. Note that only the feet and lowest parts of the legs of these figures were actually preserved.

Fig. 7. Photograph of the fragments of the Cup-Bearer, as discovered in 1900 lying fallen on the ground. The face fragment is visible in the top right quadrant of the photograph.

Gilliéron fils) which resulted in the vivid reconstruction (or "reconstitution", as Evans liked to call it) of Knossian fresco scenes and other aspects of Knossian art, often from small and isolated fragments. Indeed, it would not be going too far to say that most of the familiar Knossos fresco images which we think of as the among the greatest glories of Minoan art are arguably as much the work of the Gilliérons, working under the stimulus of their own and Evans's highly informed imaginations, as they ever were of any ancient Minoan artist.

One of the most familiar images, which seems particularly to have caught Evans's imagination and engaged his emotions, is that of the so-called Priest-King, or Prince of the Lily Crown, which he dated on stylistic grounds to Late Minoan IA (ca. 1550–1500 BC), the period of the later Palace. By the time Evans published the first volume of his great four-volume work, *The Palace of Minos at Knossos,* in 1921, the Priest-King had a central role. He was the ruler of Knossos, one of a series of dynastic Minoses analogous to the Egyptian Pharaohs, the bearer of a divine title and regarded as of divine parentage, the adopted Son on earth of the Cretan Great Mother or Earth Goddess. In this, Evans was heavily influenced by the pervasive ideas of his time about the nature of ancient religion and kingship, which reached their most comprehensive expression in the work of scholars like Sir James Frazer, in which a universal Great Goddess was attended by a dying and rising male god who symbolised the agricultural cycle and provided a divine basis for primitive kingship. His Knossian priest-king rulers were seen as the equivalents of Attis, the youthful consort of the Phrygian goddess Cybele, or of Adonis the consort of Aphrodite. The physical image of one of

Greece was not reached till the fifth century before our era, some eight or nine centuries later than the date of this Knossian fresco" (Fig. 8).[5]

The Cup-Bearer was carefully lifted by means of a laborious process of undercutting and plastering under the back, a technique which was adopted for other large fresco fragments found at Knossos. It also brought home to Evans the need for specialised drawing and restoration of the frescoes he was uncovering, and to this end he sent for Emile Gilliéron, a Swiss-born artist resident in Athens who had already carried out work for the French and other foreign Schools. This was the beginning of a particularly imaginative collaboration between Evans and Gilliéron (and, later, Gilliéron's son, Emile

Fig. 8. Restoration of Cup-Bearer Fresco, by E. Gilliéron père.

Fig. 9. Reconstruction of the figure of the Priest-King, by E. Gilliéron fils, 1926. Published in The Palace of Minos at Knossos, *vol. II, col. pl. XIV.*

them, he believed, was preserved in the relief fresco of a figure wearing a plumed lily crown and perhaps leading a sacral griffin, which was discovered at the principal approach to the Central Court from the south. This image is most familiar to us from the coloured restoration made by Emile Gilliéron fils in 1926, which was first published as the frontispiece to the second volume of *The Palace of Minos at Knossos* (Fig. 9).[6]

The extent of Evans's engagement with the figure of the Priest-King may be judged not only from the fact that he borrowed a version of the restored motif of his plumed lily crown as an embossed "logo" for the covers of the volumes of *The Palace of Minos*

at Knossos, but from his actually experiencing a vision of him. One hot night, in the grip of a mild fever (the year is not recorded, but it was probably sometime around 1905),[7] he tells of sleeping out under the observation tower erected on the eastern edge of the Central Court, close to the Grand Staircase. During the night, he awoke to find the Court bathed in warm moonlight, and looking down the well of the staircase it seemed to him that "the whole place seemed to awake awhile to life and movement. Such was the force of the illusion that the Priest-King with his plumed lily crown, great ladies, tightly girdled, flounced and corseted, long-stoled priests, and after them a retinue of elegant but sinewy youths ... passed and repassed on the flights below".[8]

In fact, however, the image of the Priest-King relief fresco, as it has come down to us through the restorations of the younger Gilliéron and his father, is arguably one of the most inventive of all the fresco images with which Knossos has been retrospectively adorned through the power of Evans's and his assistants' imaginations. The fragments around which it was created were discovered, without much obvious excitement, over a

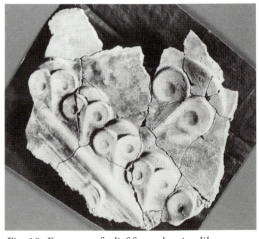

Fig. 10. Fragment of relief fresco showing lily crown.

period of nearly a week during the second season of excavations, between Saturday 11th and Friday 17th May, 1901, scattered through a basement deposit which extended between 0.30m and 2m or more from the surface in the Southern Wing of the Palace, roughly at the point where a corridor appeared to have run northward from the southern entrance into the Central Court. The discovery of the series of fragments of relief fresco is meticulously recorded by Evans's assistant, Duncan Mackenzie, in his Daybook entries for that week,[9] but Evans himself makes no mention of them in his Diary for 1901, and they do not seem to have made much impression on him at the time. In his report of the 1901 season, published in the *Annual of the British School at Athens*, Evans describes the fragments as "representing male subjects…The first important piece brought to light showed the back and ear of a male head wearing a crown [Fig. 10], the upper part of which consisted of a row of sloping *fleur-de-lys* with a taller upright one in the centre…The colours of the diadem itself and its offshoots were evidently intended to represent inlaid metal-work…It is probable that a part of a relief of a blue mantle with curving folds, crossed by fine wavy incised lines [Fig. 11], which was found near it, belonged to the same figure." A male torso found nearby with a collar of *fleur-de-lys* ornament round its neck (Fig. 12) was described as belonging to another figure, whose "attitude and clenched hand may suggest a boxer". "In addition to other minor fragments, the thigh and the greater part of the leg of another figure were also found near the torso."[10]

Initially, Evans thus evidently regarded these fragments as belonging to at least three separate male figures, and aside from noting

Fig. 11. Cast of reconstructed fragments of relief fresco incised with fine lines, originally interpreted as the folds of a blue mantle, later restored as feathered plumes attached to the top of the lily crown.

a presumption that the crowned head belonged to an image of a Mycenaean[11] King, he seems to have made little more of them at the time. Their coalescence into the figure of the highly symbolic Priest-King, which emerges fully fledged in its elaborate ideological context twenty years later in *The Palace of Minos at Knossos*, seems to have been a gradual process.[12]

The first attempts at restoration of these fragments into a single figure were made by the elder Gilliéron, probably by or in 1905 when Evans's series of graphic visions took shape.[13] In his final account of the Priest-

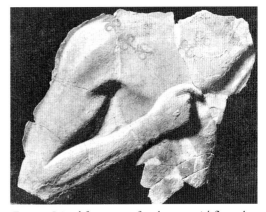

Fig. 12. Joined fragments of male torso with fleur-de-lys *ornament round its neck* (Annual of the British School at Athens 7 (1900-01), 17, fig. 6).

Fig. 13. Drawing of seal impression with portrait head of adult male, used by E. Gilliéron père to reconstruct the face of the Priest-King (cf. Fig. 14) (The Palace of Minos at Knossos I, fig. 2:a).

King relief, published in the second volume of *The Palace of Minos at Knossos*, Evans tells us that Gilliéron père originally restored the missing face of the figure in relief, along the lines of a portrait head of an adult male of "proto-Armenoid" type, with waved hair and a decidedly aquiline nose represented on a sealing of earlier date found elsewhere in the Palace (Fig. 13).[14] However, he continues, the realisation, on the grounds of the small part of forehead preserved underneath the lily crown, that the face had probably been executed "on the flat", led the younger Gilliéron to reject this element of the restoration and modify the face accordingly. Sure enough, the earliest images of the restored figure, attributable to the elder Gilliéron, show a face in low relief with a recognisable similarity to that on the sealing. A colour transparency of one of them (most probably that mentioned by Burrows) is preserved in the Ashmolean (Fig. 14). This restoration seems

first to have been illustrated by G. Maraghiannis in 1915,[15] and shows the figure composed of the same fragments and in basically the same pose as in the younger Gilliéron's 1926 reconstruction, made after the death of his father in 1924. The background, however, is a plain dark red colour, and the figure's left arm, instead of extending downwards behind him, is bent upwards at the elbow and grasps a long staff. Another version, first illustrated by H. Bossert in 1921,[16] shows much the same figure, though with greater painted detail added on the "filled in" bits. In this case, however, the lower part of the figure is set against a field of reconstructed lily or iris flowers on a pale background with a butterfly fluttering above it, while his bent left arm clutches a short cylindrical sceptre.[17] It thus seems clear that most of the basic elements of the constitution, pose and background of the figure in the younger Gilliéron's 1926 reconstruction had already been introduced by his father during his successive attempts at reconstruction. The changes made by Gilliéron fils – particularly the disposition of the figure's left arm – had less to do with the genuine reconstitution of extant fragments than with his (or rather, Evans's) ideas of the symbolic context in which he believed the image should be set.

Both the Gilliérons' restorations made use of all the major fragments which Evans had originally considered as belonging to three separate figures. The fragment of torso adorned with the *fleur-de-lys* necklace and distinguished by its bent right arm and curiously long, hooked thumb was set below the crown fragment, the gap bridged by a long slender neck and minimally painted face, shown turned in profile to the figure's right, with a frontal eye and (in the case of the 1926

Fig. 14. Early restoration of Priest-King, by E. Gilliéron père, ca. 1905.

13

Fig. 15. Photograph of butterfly, as restored.

reconstruction) a row of stylised black curls on the forehead. What had originally been seen as fragments of "blue mantle, with curving folds" were perfectly convincingly pressed into service as part of a long set of trailing plumes attached to the lily crown.[18] The thigh and leg fragments, which Evans had thought belonged to a third figure, were used to create the legs, set slightly apart and in profile, as though the figure were striding to its right. An isolated fragment of relief arm was used to construct the left upper arm of the figure, with the lower arm stretched out downwards in the case of the 1926 reconstruction, in contrast to its upwards bend in the elder Gilliéron's figures. The whole, in at least some versions, was set against a painted background of tall-stemmed, stylised lilies or irises, of which tiny fragments of one – or at most two – were preserved in reality, while above these, and behind the figure, fluttered an equally stylised butterfly (Fig. 15).

For all their imaginative properties, each of the features of the successively reconstructed images were based on contemporary artistic analogies which, moreover, were endowed by Evans and others with a progressively coherent and powerful series of symbolisms. This becomes particularly clear as one reads through Evans's description of the 1926 reconstruction in the second volume of *The Palace of Minos at Knossos.*[19] The figure of the youthful prince as a whole, and his curious half-profile, half-frontal stance, drew on the figure of the so-called "young prince" or "chieftain" portrayed in relief on a steatite cup uncovered by the Italians at the site of Ayia Triada (Fig. 16).[20] The rigidly clinched waistband and loincloth (only part of the rear flap of which was preserved along with a thigh fragment) was modelled on those of the ritual bull leapers in the Taureador fresco, recovered from the East Wing of the Palace also in 1901 (Fig. 17). The flowing peacock feather plumes arising from the top of the lily headdress (of which no trace remained on the original headdress fragment) were added on the analogy of the plumed crowns worn by sphinxes on Minoan and Mycenaean signet rings and ivory reliefs, as on a

Fig. 16. Figure of "Young Prince" (right) on steatite cup from Ayia Triada.

Fig. 17. Restored panel of Taureador Fresco, discovered in 1901, showing preserved waistbands and loincloths.

mirror handle from the cemetery of Zafer Papoura near Knossos excavated by Evans in 1904 (Fig. 18).[21] Since the sphinx was a sacred animal, it seemed particularly appropriate to Evans that the Priest-King, "the representative on earth of the Minoan Mother Goddess", should wear a related crown. The "Elysian blooms" through which the Priest-King strides were believed by Evans also to have sacred symbolism for the Minoans.[22] The ones restored by the Gilliérons were based on those painted on an amphora found by Evans in the so-called Isopata Royal Tomb at Knossos, also in 1904 (Fig. 19).[23] The butterfly was seen by Evans as symbolic of "the reawakening of the soul by divine grace after the short sleep of death".[24] It was thus particularly appropriate as an adjunct of a Knossian Priest-King, whose semi-divine character as son, and perhaps consort, of the Great Mother, symbol-

*Fig. 18. Sphinx wearing plumed crown on an ivory mirror handle from Zapher Papoura Tomb 49, Knossos, excavated in 1904 (*The Prehistoric Tombs of Knossos, *fig. 69).*

Fig. 19. Restored drawing of amphora or large jar from the Isopata 'Royal Tomb', Knossos. The stylised flowers on this provided a model for those restored on the Priest-King fresco.

ised his links with another sphere. Finally, though even he drew the line at actually reconstructing it, Evans, by 1926, had come to believe that the Priest-King ought to have been leading another sacred symbol with a special relationship with the Minoan Goddess, the griffin;[25] and to this end Gilliéron fils altered the left arm to stretch downwards behind the figure in suggestive fashion and reconstructed the left hand of the figure clutching the end of a cord which we are to imagine attached to the divine monster's neck. In a wonderful piece of joined-up imagination Evans continues by drawing a link with the griffins painted on the walls of the Knossos Throne Room in which, he suggests, the Knossian Priest-King "may well have held small consistories", with the Griffin again playing a leading part.[26]

The younger Gilliéron's reconstruction of the Priest-King relief incorporating the original fragments can today be seen – minus the "Elysian blooms" and butterfly (which seem eventually to have been rejected as too fanciful for at least some purposes) – in the Archaeological Museum in Heraklion, while a reproduction was placed in the Palace itself, on the wall of a restored section of the South-North Corridor (Fig. 20).[27] The Ashmolean possesses three copies of two versions of the restored image, both by the younger Gilliéron: two full-size plaster reproductions, one of which faithfully follows the 1926 reconstruction reproduced in *The Palace of Minos at Knossos*, and another with some differences of detail. Both were made in Oxford,[28] on the basis of different Gilliéron drawings, probably by W.H. Young, who was employed by the Ashmolean until his retirement in the late 1930s, and who acted as Evans's "formatore" in the reconstruction or reproduction of a number of Cretan or Knossian artefacts, including the plaster replica of the Throne (with an admirable sense of humour, Young often signed his replicas with the Greek word νέος, a word which means both "new" and "young"). The occasion may well have been the large Minoan Exhibition which Evans organised at Burlington House in 1936; and one of these full-scale replicas can be glimpsed, behind a glass frame, in a photograph of the Exhibition.[29] The other is a hitherto unpublished, unframed water-colour drawing, which, like the second plaster replica, differs in minor details (including the background colour against which the figure's legs are set) from the published drawing (Fig. 21). It is unsigned and undated, but we can be pretty sure that the younger Gilliéron was responsible for it, since it, too, shows the

*Fig. 20. Photograph of restored section of South-North Corridor, with replica of Priest-King (*The Palace of Minos at Knossos *II, suppl. pl. XXIX).*

Fig. 21. Unpublished reconstruction drawing of the Priest-King, probably by E. Gilliéron fils before 1926.

Fig. 22. Proposed reconstruction of the Priest-King relief as three separate figures, by W.-D. Niemeier (Mitteilungen des deutschen archäologischen Instituts, athenische Abteilung 102 (1987), 95, fig. 25; reproduced by kind permission of the author).

downward stretching left arm and the cord for leading the imaginary griffin. However, the pale background running all the way across and the relative shortness of the flower stems – together with the absence of peacock "eyes" on the plumes – bring this reconstruction somewhat closer to that of the elder Gilliéron illustrated in 1921, and it seems reasonable to suppose that it it is a little earlier than the 1926 reconstruction.

Since Evans's day, continual doubts have been expressed – on one ground or another – about his image of the Priest-King. On intellectual grounds, thinking has moved on, and the ingenious web of Minoan religion and symbolism based on earlier views of a universal Mother Goddess and her semi-divine Son, to which Evans's Priest-King was central, no longer seems as uncontroversial or persuasive as it once may have done. The reconstructed image has also been questioned on more practical artistic and archaeological grounds. One scholar has even challenged the identification of the figure as male, and has proposed restoring it as a "Princess of the Bull-Ring" leading a bull into the arena,[30]

while another has suggested reviving Evans's original idea of a boxer.[31] Many have pointed out the awkwardness with which the various elements of the final reconstruction are linked together and (rather unfairly, in view of the stylised poses often seen in genuinely preserved Minoan art) the anatomical difficulties of the reconstructed pose, while others have proposed returning to the three separate figures originally envisaged by Evans, apportioning the torso to one figure (who in this case faces to his left rather than his right and grasps a staff as in the elder Gilliéron's reconstruction), the leg and thigh fragments to another figure, who approaches the first figure, and the lily crown to a sphinx, with the "Elysian blooms" and the butterfly now banished from the picture altogether (Fig. 22).[32] In the last resort, however, these proposed reconstructions differ little in the methods they employ from those used by Evans and the Gilliérons. Though the efforts of later scholars may be based on a quantitative difference in terms of the increased number of artistic parallels and analogies now available from the Minoan world to

19

draw on, they are qualitatively the same in the sense that they too make use of precisely the kind of informed imagination which characterised the earlier reconstructions, and draw equally on explicit or unspoken assumptions about the nature and meaning of the image which may have been portrayed. They cannot, on their own, be said to tell us anything genuinely new about Minoan art and iconography, and it is hard, in all honesty, to find much if any truly objective ground on which to choose between them and the Gilliérons' versions. Meanwhile, the familiar figure of the Priest-King strides on, a compelling and evocative icon of the Minoan civilisation discovered and reshaped by Arthur Evans in the early decades of the twentieth century, and a tangible emblem of his overwhelming desire not only to reconstitute and redecorate the Palace which he began to unearth one hundred years ago but to people it once more with living beings whose ways of thought he also believed could be restored and understood.

Further Reading

Excellent accounts of the years between Evans's first visit to Knossos and the beginning of his excavations in 1900 can be found in Ann Brown's two books, *Before Knossos ... Arthur Evans's travels in the Balkans and Crete* (1993), and *Arthur Evans and the Palace of Minos* (1986), and in Joan Evans's biography of her half-brother, *Time and Chance* (1943). Information about Schliemann's interest in Knossos can be found in David Traill, *Schliemann of Troy* (1995).

An account of the discoveries of the first season at Knossos can be found in *Annual of the British School at Knossos* 6 (1899-1900), 4-70, and of the discovery of the Priest-King fragments in 7 (1900-01), 14-16. Evans's description of the Priest-King is in *The Palace of Minos at Knossos*, vol. II (1928), 774-95. Other useful discussions of this fresco are provided by N. Momigliano and M.S.F. Hood, *Annual of the British School at Athens* 89 (1994), 142-6, by W.-D. Niemeier, *Mitteilungen des deutschen archäologischen Instituts, athenische Abteilung* 102 (1987), 65-97 where two of each of the Gilliérons' reconstructions are illustrated on pl. 8, and in A. Farnoux, *Knossos: Searching for the Legendary Palace of King Minos* (1996), 130-1. The evolution of Evans's ideas concerning the role and nature of the Priest-King are analysed by E.L. Bennett, *Kretika Chronika* 15-16 (1961-62), 327-35.

Notes

1 Letter from J.L. Myres to Arthur Evans, written at the Hotel "Krete", Canea and dated 8th August, 1893. Ashmolean Museum, A.J. Evans Correspondence Volume 3. For an account of Myres's 1893 visit to Crete and his aspirations to dig at Knossos, see Ann Brown, "'I propose to begin at Gnossos'" *Annual of the British School at Athens* 81 (1986), 37-44.

2 That Evans's political track record and sympathies and his potential influence were fully appreciated by the Cretans is shown by a letter of recommendation written on his behalf by the Bishop of Hiera and Siteia in 1898 to the secular and religious authorities in the Siteia region (Ashmolean Museum, A.J. Evans Archive, Miscellaneous Documents, Box 1, no. 0187). In it, the Bishop commends Evans's credentials as a friend of the Greek nation and champion of Cretan archaeology and the Cretan Christian population, and adds that he has the ability to benefit Siteia and Crete in general, if approached in the right way.

3 Evans's close involvement with Cretan politics and international diplomacy in this period is demonstrated by his possession of a draft copy of suggested rules for the governance of a nominally independent Crete drawn up after the revolt of late summer 1896 by the Italian, French, British, Russian and Austro-Hungarian consuls in Chania (Ashmolean Museum, A.J. Evans Archive, Miscellaneous Documents, Box 1, no. 0182).

4 *Annual of the British School at Athens* 6 (1899-1900), 13.

5 *Annual of the British School at Athens* 6 (1899-1900), 15-16. Even as early as this, Evans was not far out in his estimation of the likely date of this fresco. Although the precise stratigraphical and chronological context of the deposit in which they were found must still have been uncertain in 1900, the fact that the Procession Fresco and the Cup-Bearer still remained on the walls at the time of the final destruction of the Palace in the early 14th century BC means that they were probably painted sometime between c. 1450 and c. 1400 BC, almost exactly nine centuries before 500 BC.

6 A.J. Evans, *The Palace of Minos at Knossos*, vol. II, col. pl. XIV.

7 Evans seems to have had visions of the former inhabitants of the Palace very much on his mind in that particular year. In an article in *The Times*, published on 31st October, he gives an account of the reconstitution of the Grand Staircase in terms of its inevitable appeal "to the historic sense of the most unimaginative": "..there rise before us the Grand Staircase and columnar hall of approach practically unchanged since they were traversed 32 millennia back by kings and queens of Minos's stock on their way to the more private quarters of the Royal household. We have here all the materials for the reconstruction of a brilliant picture of that remote epoch ... the low convenient balustrades that accompany the stairs, tier upon tier, upon which, as in the miniature frescoes from the North Hall of the Palace, we seem to see the Court ladies in their brilliant modern costume with pinched waists and puffed sleeves seated in groups and exchanging glances with elegant youths in the court below – dark-eyed these, with dark, flowing locks, sinewy, bronzed and bare of limb save for the tightly-drawn metal belt and ornaments, and their richly embroidered loin-cloths. A note of mystery is added by the window ... in the wall to the right ... Here surely – if fancy may indeed transport her to a sublunary scene – at times may have looked out that Princess of most ancient romance whose name is indissolubly linked with the memories of Minoan Knossos". (*The Times*, 31st October, 1905; quoted in Ann Brown, *Arthur Evans and the Palace of Knossos* (1986), 81-2.)

8 *The Palace of Minos at Knossos*, vol. III, 301.

9 Duncan Mackenzie, Daybook 1901, vol. 2, pp. 23-4, 26, 28, 30. The pieces detailed by Mackenzie are as follows: "fragments in fresco relief of the full size leg of a male? human figure with other fragments having drapery in relief" (p. 23); "a fragment of drapery in relief similar to that found Saturday evening" (p. 24); "part of the arm with right hand ... [which] was found to fit on to and explain a fragment of the shoulder found on Saturday ... [and] ... at the same place ... another large fragment ... [which] ... was found to represent in relief a fleur de lys crown in white and blue on a red ground. The ear of the head to which the crown belonged adhered but the face itself was broken away" (p. 26); "small fragments of the fresco relief" (p. 28); "stucco ... plain red without any design" (p. 30). The fragments of the crown were dealt with in the same manner as the Cup-Bearer, with plaster being applied before it was lifted. From his account, it appears that Mackenzie assumed that the fragments belonged to a single figure.

[10]   *Annual of the British School at Athens* 7 (1900-01), 15-16.

[11]   At this early stage of the excavations, Evans continued to follow contemporary archaeological convention by using the term "Mycenaean" to refer to the prehistoric antiquities he was uncovering on Crete, despite the fact that he himself had already proposed calling them "Minoan" as early as 1896, four years before he started excavating at Knossos (letter published in *The Academy*, June 20th, 1896, quoted by Joan Evans, *Time and Chance* (1943), 320). It was only from 1902 onwards that he and Duncan Mackenzie began to use "Minoan" officially, first of all as a descriptive term for Knossian pottery which they recognised as earlier in date than the Mycenaean known from the Greek mainland, and then as a distinguishing name for the Bronze Age culture of Crete in general.

[12]   Evans's first mention of the term "Priest-King" for the ruler of Knossos appears in his report of the excavations of 1903 (*Annual of the British School at Athens* 9 (1902-3), 38, 128).

[13]   In 1907, R.M. Burrows (*The discoveries in Crete*, 19) reported that "M. Gilliéron has now convincingly restored from fragments ... a life-size figure of one who must surely have been one of the Minoan Kings themselves. On his head is a crown with peacock plume, and his long flowing hair hangs down upon the fleur-de-lys chain that stretches, like some insignia, from shoulder to shoulder along the chest" (quoted by W.-D. Niemeier, "Das Stuckrelief des 'Prinzen mit der Federkrone'" *Mitteilungen des deutschen archäologischen Instituts, athenische Abteilung* 102 (1987), 71).

[14]   *The Palace of Minos at Knossos*, vol. II, 779. The sealing from which the elder Gilliéron drew his inspiration is illustrated in vol. I, 8, fig. 2:a.

[15]   G. Maraghiannis, *Antiquités crétoises III* (1915), pl. 9.

[16]   H. Bossert, *Altkreta* (1921), fig. 74 (fig. 78 in the 1923 edn.).

[17]   A third Gilliéron père reconstruction – somewhat earlier than this – was illustrated in H.R. Hall, *The ancient history of the Near East* (1913), pl. 4.1. It is very similar to the one illustrated by Bossert, except that the butterfly is reconstructed as another flower.

[18]   Although the "blue mantle" fragments were already restored in this way in the elder Gilliéron's first reconstruction, a note added by Mackenzie in his 1901 Day-book to the effect that these "drapery" fragments were really feathers belonging to the crown worn by the figure is, curiously, dated August 1918.

[19]   *The Palace of Minos at Knossos*, vol. II, 774-95.

[20]   *The Palace of Minos at Knossos*, vol. II, 790-2, fig. 516. The influence of this figure is particularly clear in the elder Gilliéron's reconstruction of the figure holding a long staff.

[21]   *The Palace of Minos at Knossos*, vol. II, 777-9, fig. 506. The peacock feather eyes, shown clearly at the ends of the plumes on the younger Gilliéron's published reconstruction, of which Evans (*ibid.*, 777) claims that one was actually preserved, are a pure figment of the imagination. Not only do peacocks appear to have been unknown in the Near East and Egypt – let alone further west – before the first millennium BC (they are native to the Indian sub-continent), but no such feature was preserved on any of the original fragments, and the eyes appear only on this and the reconstruction now in the Heraklion Museum, also by Gilliéron fils. The most likely candidate for exotic plumes in this period would be ostrich feathers.

[22]   The iris, in particular, is the flower associated with Hyakinthos, with whom, in Classical mythology, Apollo fell in love. The ending -inthos betrays a pre-Greek name, and the myth of Hyakinthos may perhaps have had its origins in some Cretan vegetation god. Evans had earlier discussed the religious symbolism of the iris in *The Mycenaean Tree and Pillar Cult and its Mediterranean Relations* (1901), 49-50.

[23]   *The Palace of Minos at Knossos*, vol. II, 786-7, 789; cf. A.J. Evans, *The Prehistoric Tombs of Knossos* (1905), pl. CI.

[24]   *The Palace of Minos at Knossos*, vol II, 787-90. In *The Ring of Nestor: a glimpse into the Minoan after-world* (1925), 53-64, Evans elaborates this symbolism of the butterfly at much greater length.

[25]   Evans's conviction in this respect was encouraged by the portrayal of what he regarded as a priest leading a griffin by a cord on a sealstone from a tomb at Vaphio in southern Greece, excavated in the late 1880s (cf. *The Palace of Minos at Knossos* II, 785, fig. 512).

[26]   *The Palace of Minos at Knossos*, vol. II, 785.

[27]   Cf. Evans, *The Palace of Minos at Knossos*, vol. II, 795, suppl. pl. XXIX.

28 The moulds used to reproduce the relief elements are still in the Ashmolean.

29 See Ann Brown, *Arthur Evans and the Palace of Minos* (1986), pl. 2. The head of the framed Priest King is just visible on the righthand wall, a few feet beyond the replica of the Throne.

30 M. Cameron, "New restorations of Minoan Frescoes from Knossos" *Bulletin of the Institute of Classical Studies* 17 (1970), 164; cf. also, more recently, E.N. Davis, in *The Role of the Ruler in the Prehistoric Aegean*, ed. Paul Rehak, 1995, 12-13. This is on the grounds of the comparatively pale colour of the torso which, it is suggested, represents the white usually used for female flesh rather than the reddish hue normally associated with males, such as the Cup-Bearer (Fig. 8). However, Evans himself was in no doubt right from the start (and

long before the Priest-King himself took shape) that the fragments belonged to what he then considered to be at least three *male* figures, and expressed his belief that the skin was originally coloured a reddish brown, but that the surface had faded as a result of long burial in the ground. The most that can be said is that the colour of the fragments in their preserved state seems ambiguous (Fig. 14): it could be a much stained white or a faded reddish brown.

31 J. Coulomb, "Le 'prince aux lis' de Knosos reconsidéré" *Bulletin de Correspondance hellénique* 103 (1979), 29-50.

32 See especially W.-D. Niemeier, "Das Stuckrelief des Prinzen mit der Federkrone" *Mitteilungen des deutschen archäologischen Instituts, athenische Abteilung* 102 (1987), 65-97, figs. 24-6.

ISBN I 85444 142 6

British Library Catalogue-in-Publication data: A catalogue record of this book is available from the British Library.

Cover illustration: Reconstruction of the figure of the Priest-King by E. Gilliéron fils, 1926 (fig.9)

Designed by Andrew Ivett and typeset in Garamond

Printed in England by Stanley L. Hunt (Printers) Ltd, Rushden, Northamptonshire